THIS CREATIVE
SPACE BELONGS TO:

NAME:

ADDRESS:

EMAIL:

TELEPHONE:

BEAR IN MIND

Bear in mind that this journal belongs to you. All the things you discover within its pages are waiting for you to take ownership of them. You may do with them as the mood takes you. You can choose to read or observe them, edit or amend them, deface or destroy them, meditate with them or completely ignore them. The more you do, the more the journal will become a part of you, and you a part of it. It will blossom into your own creative space, and grow into a uniquely personal record.

Bear in mind that you are in complete control when you enter this journal. Your creative space is filled with over 100 tasks and projects, ideas and inspirations, sparks and nudges. They are intended as catalysts, designed to add art and mischief to your world. The spaces, frames, lines, and bullets around them are there to be commandeered by you. They are places where you can dream, scheme, invent, imagine, write, list, draw, paint, fold, glue, and do anything that will fit within the pages.

Bear in mind that sometimes you won't want to bear anything in mind. If you need a little breathing space, you can also use your journal to clear your mind completely.

"THE WORLD IS BUT A CANVAS
TO OUR IMAGINATION."

–Henry David Thoreau

A CREATIVE SPACE JOURNEY

Your journal has been designed and constructed to encourage you to use the advanced scientific method of "doing something rather than nothing." This has, over time, proven itself to be the main factor in creating anything. As Picasso once said: "Inspiration exists, but it has to find you working."

The ideas within the journal are there to help your imagination and inventiveness flourish. Their aim is to make you think a little differently; and, who knows, perhaps travel to places you wouldn't ordinarily travel. Fill your creative space with thoughts, stories, pictures, and photographs. It doesn't matter how good they are. What matters is that you are doing something creative.

The tasks are separated into "moods" by the tabs that run along the edge of the pages. Some tasks are designed to enhance your mood, others to change it. The task-to-mood connection is just a guide. Try picking out a page at random or choosing the opposite mood to the one you are in, and see what happens. You can work through the journal from beginning to end if you prefer, the choice is yours.

We would love to see what you come up with, so please photograph and post your drawings, lists, creations, and scribbles on social media using **#creativespacejournal**. We wish you the best of luck on your journey, and hope your journal might help you to float up into a creative space where you discover something incredible.

CREATIVITIES

Tick off your creative adventures

	14	HIGH-FIVE EXPERIMENT
	16	INKBLOTS
	19	FINGERPRINT PET
	20	BEST FRIEND EXPERIMENT
	21	MIRROR, MIRROR
	22	SINGING EXPERIMENT
	24	MOLECULE METAMORPHOSIS
	26	MODEL CITIZEN
	27	BREATHING SPACE
	29	CAT SCAN
	31	GLASSES HALF FULL
	32	A TO Z OF HAPPY
	33	CREATIVE SPACE
	34	GALLERY EXPERIMENT
	35	PLANT PROJECT
	36	STOP! (AND SMELL THE ROSES)
	38	IF WISHES WERE BULLETS
	39	MIRROR, MIRROR
	40	GETTING PERSONAL
	41	BREATHING SPACE
	42	TIME TRAVEL EXPERIMENT
	44	UNICORN EXERCISE
	45	NO, NO, NO
	47	OBITUARY PROJECT
	48	COLOR PROFILE
	49	CREATIVE SPACE

	51	FURIOUS SCRIBBLE
	53	TAKE A BREAK
	54	CREATIVE DESTRUCTION
	55	ANGRY ACTIVITY
	56	BAD REVIEW
	57	MIRROR, MIRROR
	59	COFFEE SHOP CALM
	60	PASSIVE-AGGRESSIVE HUMMING
	61	BETTER OUT THAN IN
	62	POSITIVE THINKING
	63	BREATHING SPACE
	64	PRIMAL SCREAM
	65	CREATIVE SPACE
	66	999 CRANES
	67	MIRROR, MIRROR
	69	FRAMING EXERCISE
	70	BREATHING SPACE
	71	BRAIN IN A JAR
	72	SURREALIST HEAD SPACE
	74	PIPE EXPERIMENT
	75	IDEAS IDEA
	76	STILL LIFE
	77	BRAINWAVES
	79	ALIEN CONCEPT
	80	SOCK PEOPLE
	81	CREATIVE SPACE

■ HAPPY		■ ANGRY		■ PLAYFUL		■ WIRED
■ SAD		■ RELAXED		■ BORED		■ SLEEPY

82	DOG EXPERIMENT
84	BEST BEASTIES
85	MIRROR, MIRROR
86	ZINE PROJECT
88	FACE EXPERIMENT
90	WHAT THE BOINK?
91	LETTING GO
92	EAVESDROP EXPERIMENT
93	DEADLINE HEADLINE
94	PATHS OF DESIRE
95	BREATHING SPACE
96	SHERLOCKING
97	CREATIVE SPACE
98	TICKET PROJECT
99	10 FANTASY JOURNEYS
100	BROKEN FRIENDSHIPS
101	MIND MAZE
102	ALMOST FAMOUS
103	MIRROR, MIRROR
104	DRAINING EXERCISE
105	WILD PET PORTRAIT
107	MEMORY EXPERIMENT
108	10 FAVORITE MOVIES
109	BREATHING SPACE
110	FACE PAINT
111	CREATIVE SPACE

113	ANIMAL FRIENDS
114	RUDE EXERCISE
115	10 NAUGHTY THOUGHTS
116	LIAR, LIAR
117	WRITE DOWN A SECRET
118	UPSIDE-DOWNER
119	MIRROR, MIRROR
120	PYRAMID TALES
122	TATTOO HUNT
123	BREATHING SPACE
124	TIGHT SQUEEZE
126	DISPOSABLE ART
127	CREATIVE SPACE
129	POSITION PROJECT
130	MIRROR, MIRROR
131	LISTLESS
133	DREAM PROJECT
134	HIBERNATION
135	BREATHING SPACE
136	MUSICAL IMPROVISATION
137	SLEUTH EXERCISE
138	IMPOSSIBLE TASK
140	MARS MISSION
141	COFFEE TIME
142	COUNTING SHEEP
143	CREATIVE SPACE

A YEAR OF CREATIVITY

Keep a record of the creative activities, or "creativities," you do each week for a year, and how they make you feel. You can then look back in the future on the record of your creative space travels.

WEEK	DATE	PAGE	CREATIVITY	MOOD NOTES
1				
2				
3				
4				
5				
6				
7				
8				
9				
10				
11				
12				
13				

WEEK	DATE	PAGE	CREATIVITY	MOOD NOTES
14				
15				
16				
17				
18				
19				
20				
21				
22				
23				
24				
25				
26				

WEEK	DATE	PAGE	CREATIVITY	MOOD NOTES
27				
28				
29				
30				
31				
32				
33				
34				
35				
36				
37				
38				
39				

WEEK	DATE	PAGE	CREATIVITY	MOOD NOTES
40				
41				
42				
43				
44				
45				
46				
47				
48				
49				
50				
51				
52				

A CREATIVE WEEK

Select at random seven creativities to do in a week.
Do one a day and keep a note of your moods and discoveries.
You can copy this template for creating future plans and logs of
your creative space travel.

DAY	CREATIVITY	PAGE	MOOD NOTES
MONDAY			
TUESDAY			
WEDNESDAY			

DAY	CREATIVITY	PAGE	MOOD NOTES
THURSDAY			
FRIDAY			
SATURDAY			
SUNDAY			

HIGH-FIVE EXPERIMENT

Ask someone passing you on the street for a high-five.
Respect their right to refuse.

5 REASONS TO HIGH-FIVE

INKBLOTS

Draw what you see in the inkblots.

Monday

Tuesday

Thursday

Friday

FINGERPRINT PET

Create your own print pet every day for a week.

Wednesday

Saturday

Sunday

BEST FRIEND EXPERIMENT

Treat everyone you meet today as your best friend.
Write about your day.

MIRROR, MIRROR

Look at yourself in a mirror when you're happy.
Draw a portrait of your happy self.
Give them a name.

SINGING EXPERIMENT

Listen to music while walking along the street, and sing along loudly.
Notice the reactions of others. Draw their facial expressions.

MOLECULE METAMORPHOSIS

If you weren't a human, what would you rather be?
Draw 5 creatures or objects that you wouldn't mind
your molecules morphing into.

MODEL CITIZEN

Make as many small animals as you can out of sticky tack or molding compound.
Leave them in places where they will give people a nice surprise.

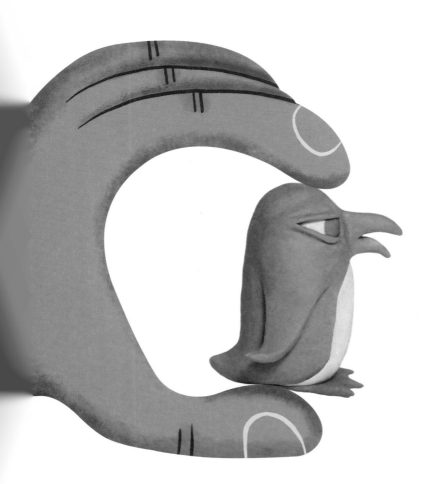

BREATHING SPACE

Whenever you visit this page, close
your eyes and take 5 minutes away
from the world. Allow your mind to
focus on nothing but your breathing.

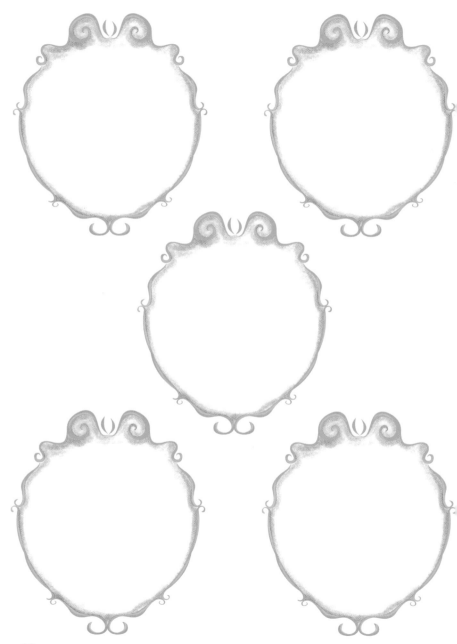

CAT SCAN

Photograph the faces of all the cats that you meet this week.
Draw them and give them names.

ESMERELDA

GLASSES HALF FULL

Draw the faces to match the glasses.

A TO Z OF HAPPY

Write an A to Z of things that make you smile.

A ....

B ....

C ....

D ....

E ....

F ....

G ....

H ....

I ....

J ....

K ....

L ....

M ....

N ....

O ....

P ....

Q ....

R ....

S ....

T ....

U ....

V ....

W ....

X ....

Y ....

Z ....

CREATIVE SPACE

We all need time to smile.
This is your happy space. Scrapbook the page with pictures
of whatever makes you feel happiest.

GALLERY EXPERIMENT

1 Choose one of your drawings from this journal.

2 Tear it out.

3 Tape it up somewhere in your home where you will see it every day.

PLANT PROJECT

Buy a plant. Talk to it every day.
Write down the things you discuss.

STOP! (AND SMELL THE ROSES)

Draw a flower on this page every day for a week. Look back at this page
every time you feel unhappy, and imagine how the flowers would smell.

Monday

Tuesday

Wednesday

Thursday

Friday

Saturday

Sunday

IF WISHES WERE BULLETS

List your 6 greatest achievements.
List 6 things you would like to achieve.

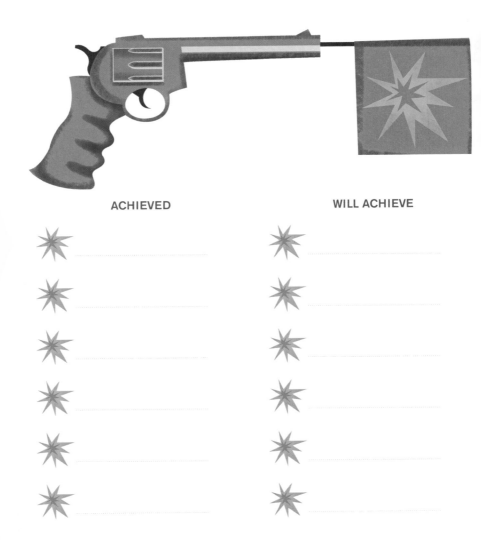

ACHIEVED

WILL ACHIEVE

MIRROR, MIRROR

Look at yourself in a mirror when you're sad.
Draw a portrait of your sad self.
Give them a name.

GETTING PERSONAL

Try not to say "me" or "I" for the entire day.

BREATHING SPACE

Whenever you visit this page, close
your eyes and take 5 minutes away
from the world. Allow your mind to
focus on nothing but your breathing.

TIME TRAVEL EXPERIMENT

Think about a specific time, in the future,
when you will think back to this moment.
Write about that future moment.

FUTURE MOMENT

UNICORN EXERCISE

Draw a body for your magical unicorn.

NO, NO, NO

Say "NO!" to anything you
don't want to do today.

OBITUARY PROJECT

Read all the obituaries in the newspaper.
Draw a comic strip of the most inspiring
life you find there.

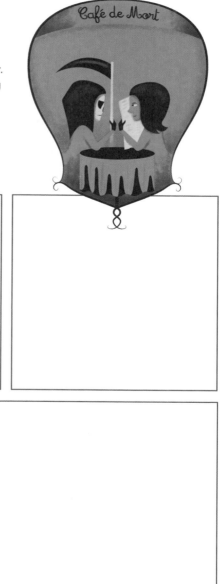

COLOR PROFILE

Draw a portrait of the most boring person you know.
Color it in using the brightest pens or paints you can find.

CREATIVE SPACE

We all need room to stop and think.
This is your sad space. Dispose of your sad thoughts here.

FURIOUS SCRIBBLE

Scribble on this page for exactly 1 minute.
Stare at what you have done for 3 minutes.
Add the features to make an angry character.

TAKE A BREAK

Inspiration often begins with failure.
Break something. Draw the pieces.

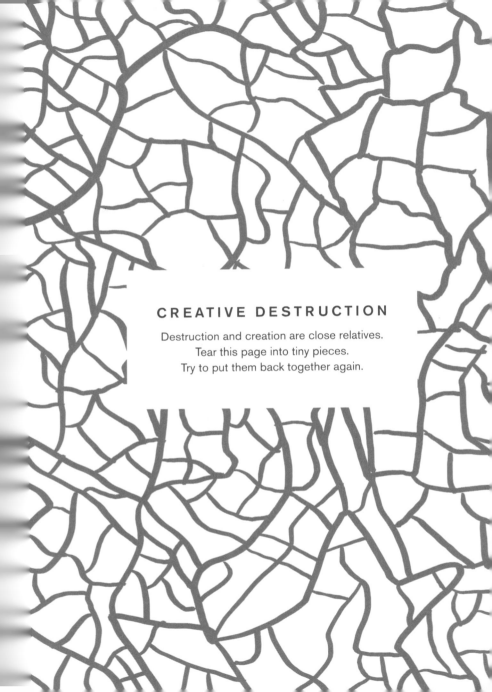

CREATIVE DESTRUCTION

Destruction and creation are close relatives.
Tear this page into tiny pieces.
Try to put them back together again.

ANGRY ACTIVITY

Write a list of 6 things that make you angry.
Cross out each one and never think of them again.

1

2

3

4

5

6

BAD REVIEW

Stand in the middle of a bookstore or library.
Look to your left and take out the second book that catches your eye.
Read it and write a scathing review.

MIRROR, MIRROR

Look at yourself in a mirror when you're angry.
Draw a portrait of your angry self.
Give them a name.

COFFEE SHOP CALM

Sit in a coffee shop for an hour and draw your surroundings.
Don't think about anything else until the time is up.

PASSIVE-AGGRESSIVE HUMMING

Hum a really annoying tune and see how many other
people you can infect with it.

BETTER OUT THAN IN

Think of your biggest bugbear or pet peeve in life.
Draw it here.

POSITIVE THINKING

Try not to say anything negative today.
Whenever you fail, write down what you said.

BREATHING SPACE

Whenever you visit this page, close
your eyes and take 5 minutes away
from the world. Allow your mind to
focus on nothing but your breathing.

PRIMAL SCREAM

Picture the most peaceful place you know.
Travel there. Shout until you are hoarse.

CREATIVE SPACE

We all need room to vent our frustrations.
This is your angry space. Use it to release your anger.

999 CRANES

Fold a square piece of paper to make a crane.
Make 998 more through your lifetime.
When you have finished you can make a wish.

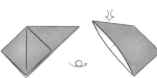

| fold to create triangle | fold upward | open top flap and tuck corners inward | turn over and repeat |

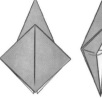

| fold top layer to center, then unfold | fold top layer upward | press sides inward at the same time | flatten | turn over and repeat |

| fold top layer to center | turn over and repeat | fold each 'leg' upward to create crease | reverse fold the 'legs' inward | fold one side to create a head |

fold down wings on each side and you're done

MIRROR, MIRROR

Look at yourself in a mirror when you're relaxed.
Draw a portrait of your sleepy self.
Give them a name.

FRAMING EXERCISE

Tear a hole in this page. Hold it up in front of you
and draw what you see through it in the frame.

Tear here

Frame

BREATHING SPACE

Whenever you visit this page, close
your eyes and take 5 minutes away
from the world. Allow your mind to
focus on nothing but your breathing.

BRAIN IN A JAR

Imagine you are nothing but a brain in a jar.
Reality is just electrical signals being fed into the jar.
Draw your brain. Draw your jar.
Think about your reality.

SURREALIST HEAD SPACE

Draw or write whatever comes to mind, without looking
down at the page, for 5 minutes.

PIPE EXPERIMENT

Realize that this is not a pipe.

IDEAS IDEA

Notice where you have your best ideas and write a list of these places.
Make a conscious effort to spend more time there.

STILL LIFE

Set up a still life and use basic shapes to help you draw the objects.

1 ....

2 ....

3 ....

4 ....

5 ....

6 ....

7 ....

8 ....

9 ....

10 ....

BRAINWAVES

Make a list of 10 songs that calm your mind.

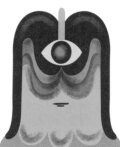

ALIEN CONCEPT

The aliens have landed. Draw their bodies.

SOCK PEOPLE

Take off both your socks and place them over your hands to make sock people.
Imagine that one of them is a pessimist and the other is an optimist: now make
them converse about the state of the world today (silly voices are optional).

CREATIVE SPACE

We all need room to chill out and be mindful.
This is your relaxed space. Fill it with calm thoughts and visit it often.

DOG EXPERIMENT

Find a picture of a dog. Fold the dog to create a fantastical creature.

AFFIX HERE

BEST BEASTIES

Mix two animals together to create a new species.
Give your species a name.

T-PECKS

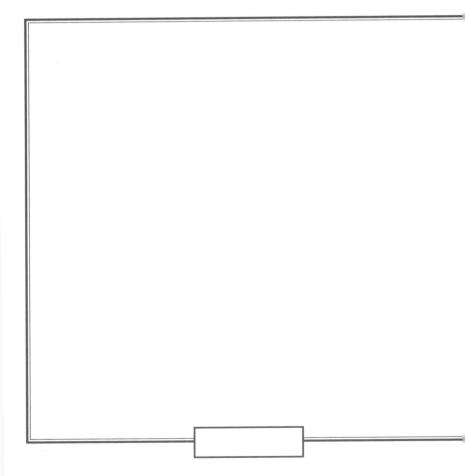

MIRROR, MIRROR

Look at yourself in a mirror when you're feeling mischievous.
Draw a portrait of your playful self.
Give them a name.

ZINE PROJECT

Trace the template. Fold and cut to make a zine. Draw the story of the best day you have ever had. Staple the zine in your journal.

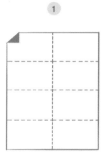

 cut

- - - - fold

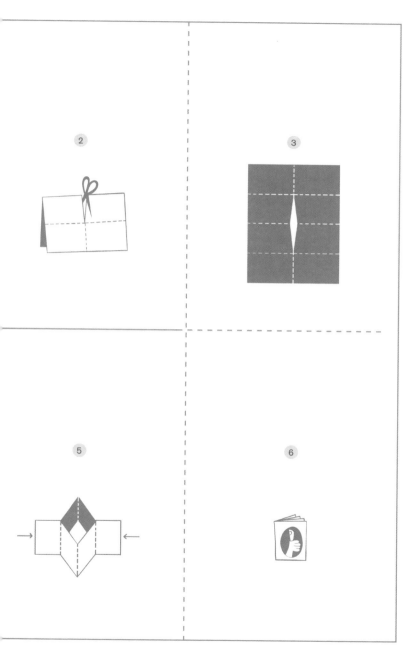

FACE EXPERIMENT

Cut out the face parts and glue them to inanimate objects.
Photograph people reacting to them.

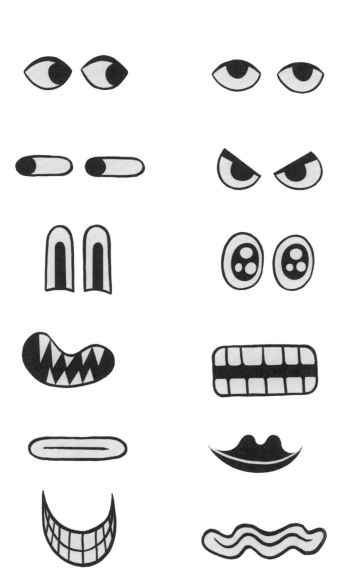

1 ....

2 ....

3 ....

4 ....

5 ....

6 ....

7 ....

8 ....

9 ....

10 ....

WHAT THE BOINK?

Invent 10 new curse words and try to use them in conversation.

LETTING GO

Write down your contact details in the box below. Mark the page.
Leave your journal in a public space. See if anyone returns it.

If found please return to:

EAVESDROP EXPERIMENT

Listen in on the conversations of strangers.
Write down what you hear.

DEADLINE HEADLINE

Fail to do something you are really supposed to do.
Notice the consequences.

Neglected Task Consequences

PATHS OF DESIRE

Vary a regular walk by veering slightly from the path.
Hop along walls, jump on benches, and walk on the grass.

BREATHING SPACE

Whenever you visit this page, close
your eyes and take 5 minutes away
from the world. Allow your mind to
focus on nothing but your breathing.

SHERLOCKING

In a public place, observe a stranger.
Write down every tiny detail that you notice about them.
Present your findings.

Observations

Conclusion

CREATIVE SPACE

We all need room to play, to joke, to make mischief.
This is your play space. Fill it with things that make you laugh.

TICKET PROJECT

Draw on your used bus or train tickets.
Leave them on the seat for other travelers to discover,
hopefully inspiring them to do the same.

10 FANTASY JOURNEYS

List 10 fantastical journeys you want to embark on.

1

2

3

4

5

6

7

8

9

10

BROKEN FRIENDSHIPS

Spend a week collecting broken and discarded objects.
Arrange the objects to make faces. Photograph your new friends
and stick your favorite one in the journal.

MIND MAZE

Design a maze and hide something
precious to you at its center.

ALMOST FAMOUS

Write a list of 10 famous people who you would
like to meet in your lifetime.

1 ....

2 ....

3 ....

4 ....

5 ....

6 ....

7 ....

8 ....

9 ....

10 ....

MIRROR, MIRROR

Look at yourself in a mirror when you're bored.
Draw a portrait of your uninterested self.
Give them a name.

DRAINING EXERCISE

Walk the streets, looking down to observe the drains and manhole covers.
Photograph them and copy the patterns.

WILD PET PORTRAIT

Go for a walk and draw a portrait of the first animal you see.
Give him or her a name.

HELEN

MEMORY EXPERIMENT

While watching a movie, doodle whatever comes into your head.
Ask a friend to review your doodles and try to name the movie.

10 FAVORITE MOVIES

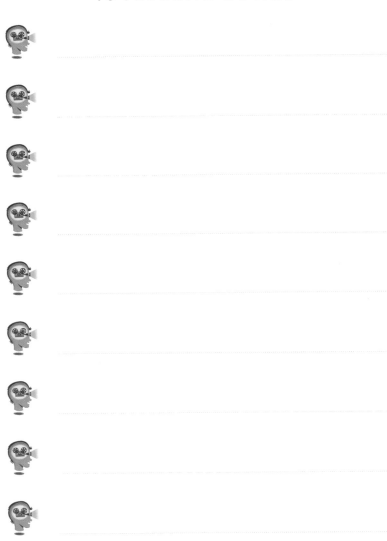

BREATHING SPACE

Whenever you visit this page, close
your eyes and take 5 minutes away
from the world. Allow your mind to
focus on nothing but your breathing.

FACE PAINT

Complete these faces to reflect your different moods.

CREATIVE SPACE

We all need room to escape our routines and rules.
This is your bored space. Visit when you're uninspired. Fill it with exciting images.

ANIMAL FRIENDS

Draw your friends as animals. Never show them the drawings.

NEVER!

RUDE EXERCISE

Draw the rudest thing you can think of.
Share it with someone.

10 NAUGHTY THOUGHTS

List the wildest ideas you have.

LIAR, LIAR

A beautiful story begins with a pack of lies.
Make something up.

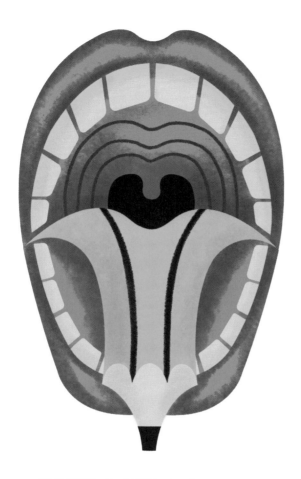

WRITE DOWN A SECRET

Tell it to as many people as you can today.

UPSIDE-DOWNER

Draw something that works both ways up.
Surround it with words that work back to front.

MIRROR, MIRROR

Look at yourself in a mirror when you're feeling wired.
Draw a portrait of your energetic self.
Give them a name.

PYRAMID TALES

Write six dramatic stories, each in five sentences, using the structure known as Freytag's Pyramid after the German novelist Gustav Freytag.

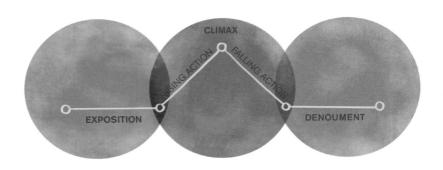

CLIMAX

RISING ACTION

FALLING ACTION

EXPOSITION

DENOUMENT

TATTOO HUNT

Keep an eye out for tattoos on the people you encounter.
Draw your favorites here.

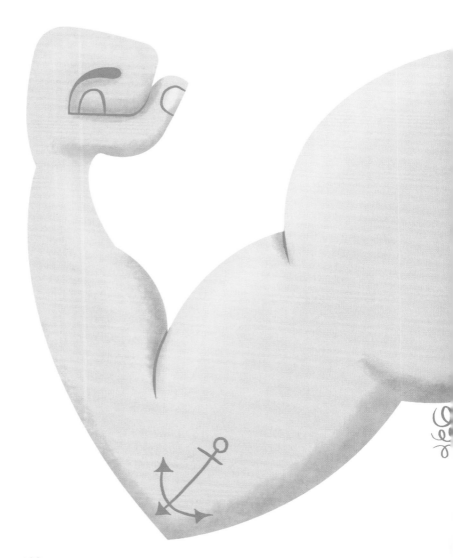

BREATHING SPACE

Whenever you visit this page, close
your eyes and take 5 minutes away
from the world. Allow your mind to
focus on nothing but your breathing.

TIGHT SQUEEZE

Draw something on this page that is far too big to live there.

DISPOSABLE ART

Spend 10 minutes every day drawing until you have filled this page.
Stare at the page until you have committed it to memory.

DESTROY IT.

CREATIVE SPACE

We all need room to run and jump and scream.
This is your wired space. Store your wildest thoughts here.

Monday

Tuesday

Saturday

POSITION PROJECT

Every day for a week, notice what position your body is in when you wake up.
Draw the positions.

Wednesday

Thursday

Friday

Sunday

MIRROR, MIRROR

Look at yourself in a mirror when you're tired.
Draw a portrait of your sleepy self.
Give them a name.

LISTLESS

Make a list of 10 things that you would
rather be doing than writing this list.

1
2
3
4
5
6
7
8
9
10

SLEEPY

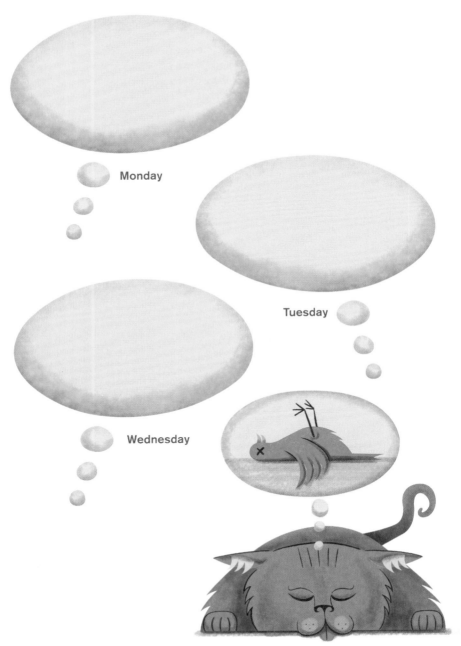

Monday

Tuesday

Wednesday

DREAM PROJECT

Keep this journal by your bed and write down
your dreams every morning for a week.
At the end of the week, read them to a friend.

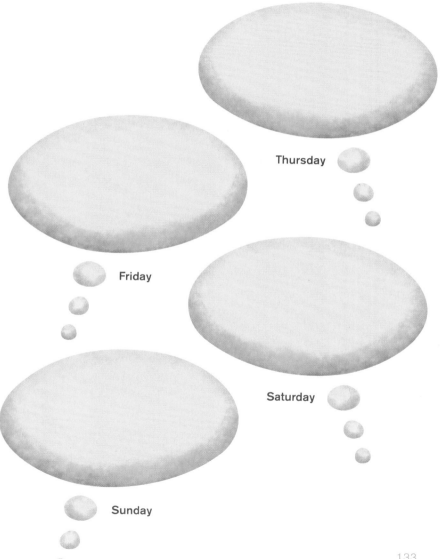

Thursday

Friday

Saturday

Sunday

133

HIBERNATION

Make a blanket fort in your living room. Take a nap in your fort
for as many days as you like.

BREATHING SPACE

Whenever you visit this page, close
your eyes and take 5 minutes away
from the world. Allow your mind to
focus on nothing but your breathing.

MUSICAL IMPROVISATION

Play a favorite piece of music. As you listen,
draw the pattern that the notes make in your head.

SLEUTH EXERCISE

While watching your favorite detective show,
draw a portrait of the sleuth.

SLEEPY

IMPOSSIBLE TASK

Notice how the corners of these shapes are impossibly connected.

WRITE A LIST OF 10 IMPOSSIBLE THINGS.

MARS MISSION

You're traveling to Mars. Design a space suit and
label its revolutionary features.

COFFEE TIME

Draw a self-portrait in the time it takes to make a hot drink.
Consider your work over a cup of coffee.

COUNTING SHEEP

Draw sheep until you fall asleep.
Count them up in the morning.

CREATIVE SPACE

We all need a place where we feel safe and secure.
This is your sleepy space. Write your dreams here to keep them safe.

STERLING
New York

1166 Avenue of the Americas
New York, NY 10036

First published in the UK in 2017 by Ammonite Press, an imprint
of Guild of Master Craftsman Publications Ltd

This Sterling edition published in 2019 by Sterling Publishing Co., Inc.

© 2017 Lucy Irving

ISBN 978-1-4549-3634-3

Distributed in Canada by Sterling Publishing Co., Inc.
c/o Canadian Manda Group, 664 Annette Street
Toronto, Ontario M6S 2C8, Canada

For information about custom editions, special sales, and premium and corporate
purchases, please contact Sterling Special Sales at 800-805-5489
or specialsales@sterlingpublishing.com.

Manufactured in Malaysia

2 4 6 8 10 9 7 5 3 1

sterlingpublishing.com

Design by Robin Shields